The Freedom of Un ..owing

The Freedom of Unknowing

communicate this perplexing message. The simplicity of unknowing is the joy of aliveness. What is being said is just energy dancing, singing and laughing; it is what is and, of course, what is not.

I can't.

'I' know. As long as there is the belief that this illusory 'I' is real, the sincere seeker cannot forget about it.

What happens when there is no more 'I' or 'me'?

Nothing, absolutely nothing; however, in the story of 'Jim', all *seeking* **stopped**. All, so-called, teachings that purported any kind of spiritual awakening were **abandoned**. *Searching* was **terminated**. The *story* of 'me' was no more!

An *indescribable* validation, a recognition, so to speak, that there *never* was a 'me' to have a story in the first place turned up.

You mean you experienced and realized there was never a 'me'?

No, it was not an experience or realization. One could imply, in a nonsensical way, "No one recognized there was never a 'me' in the first place."

Could that be called Grace?

You could call it anything, but that would not be it.

Unconditional love?

Sure, but that would not be it either, because it is impossible to describe. How do you describe nothing and everything as one word?

One could say 'This' is unconditional love sans acceptance, rejection, right or wrong.

Just 'This'?

Yes.

Stories can be tools that help to expose the illusion of 'me', but really, that's all that can be done...lay bare the illusion of 'me' over and over and, perhaps, the story can fall away.

Am 'I' Aware?

There is just 'This' unknowing.

No 'me' or 'I' to say, "Yes" or "no" to the question.

Apparent breathing, buzzing in the apparent head, the apparent feel of the chair…

Isn't that being aware?

It would take something like consciousness being aware of itself to answer, but who would know that?

Well, 'I' would know that?

The 'I' assumes the qualities of consciousness and feels secure in that assumption. The 'I' is not real and dives into apparent consciousness to preserve itself. It asserts itself as consciousness, that which is aware.

Awareness separates. One could say awareness and consciousness are one in the same, but it just does not matter.

'I' wants to survive and will use all manner of religion, philosophy, and self enquiry to ensure its immortality.

So, there is no awareness?

There is just what is happening. When one apparently becomes aware of what is just happening, separation slips in. Awareness, like a shadow, claims ownership to what's happening.

I am aware of drinking from this cool stream. I am aware of brushing my teeth. I am aware of the clouds...

Is that what you mean by duality?

When what is happening turns into, "I am aware of what is happening," yes, that is duality.

'I' wants to lay claim and knowingly be the pure light of consciousness. It will have convincing proof to make it so; curiously, the word consciousness seems to be the new word for God in many self enquiry circles.

The euphoric freedom of unknowing *lays to waste* all the wizardry of awareness, presence, being in the now, consciousness and any other word that apparently silhouettes what is simply just happening.

There is just the marvel of what is happening for no one. 'This' cannot be comprehended. It, and it's not an it, is the precious riddle.

Unknowing is probably as close to expressing what cannot be known as one can get in oral or written language.

One could say that awareness promotes or triggers separation; the simple phenomenon of what's happening gets blacked out by that which is aware.

When the illusory, dreamed-up 'I' is no more, it is impossible to black anything out. There is nothing there to be covered! Nothing to be aware!

One is the stream

laughing water roaring over apparent rocks

one is the air

whispering its delight, as it rushes through trees

one is the apparent earth

a shining blue jewel

one is nothing

arising as simple laughter.

There is nothing to separate out into an 'I' or 'me'; yet, there can be the appearance of separating into an 'I' or 'me'.

As Is

'This' is unimaginable, incomprehensible, unspeakable freedom, as is.

'This' is unimaginable because it is 'This' which is already. There is no having to imagine breathing, the apparent view from the window, elbows on the table, words appearing on this computer screen, the cars passing in the distance.

What about everything else going on in the world and universe?

Just like your question, it's what's happening. With all the technology available, it's possible to include *which is already* a million-fold, ten million-fold, a billion-fold; but it would still be **just what is happening**.

The apparent 'me' wants to know why things are the way they are, why the world is so messed up, why people are so cruel to each other. All seven billion humans seem to have a story of how things should be, or how good things used to be. However, all those stories are still just what is happening.

The 'me' tries to imagine why things are the way they are.

It's bone chillingly simple. Things are the way they are because they are.

I just don't get it.

How can you get what is already? Everyone tries to get 'This'. It's silly to try and comprehend what's happening; yet, most people try to comprehend the incomprehensible.

When the 'me' is no more, the obviousness of this communication is astounding; yet, it remains unimaginable to the 'me'.

So, if I can't imagine what 'This' is, I certainly can't comprehend it.

There is nothing to imagine and certainly nothing to comprehend. What's happening is what's happening. There is nothing to look for, it is this already.

I just can't stop looking because I still haven't found what I'm looking for.

You haven't found it because it is 'This' already. What you are looking for are the very words you are already speaking, the air you are breathing, the thoughts you are having.

It can't be as simple as you say!

The fact is, it is even more simple!

I just want to cry and hit something when you say things like that.

You want to get it, to know it, to own it, but you can't. Yes, it can be very frustrating. That's what we see so often in the apparent world. People can't have it the way they want, so they hit each other, hurt each other, wars erupt, nations fall.

'This' is unspeakable. Perhaps these words should not even be written. All that's being said cannot describe or even come close to explaining 'This' freedom.

Then why do you keep talking and writing about it?

There is no answer to that question. It's just what is happening.

As is?

Yes, as is.

Laughter

Returning to the Illusory Belief of 'Me'

Is it possible for you to return to believing 'Jim' is real again?

Is it possible to return to the belief that on December 24th Santa Claus is going to land on the roof, park his reindeer, grab his bag and slide down the chimney? Not only that, but then, know exactly what you ordered for Christmas, place it under the tree, eat the cookies you put out for him, go back up the chimney, get in his sleigh, and take off?

So, there really is no 'I' or 'me' to be aware?

Was that silver dollar you found the next morning on the windowsill, in place of the tooth you placed there, from the tooth fairy?

You mean there is no 'I' or 'me' here to be enlightened?

Were those pretty eggs you found in the grass from the Easter bunny? Were those chocolate rabbits, candy chickens, jelly beans, and fake grass in your Easter basket from a magical rabbit?

But, what about this very real 'self' that feels afraid?

Was that man everyone feared, as they ventured into the forest, the real boogeymen?

The point being made is simple and obvious. As children these beliefs are very real indeed; and then, the calamitous realization that there's no such thing as a real Santa occurs. It is now obvious there is no such thing, nor could there ever have been, nor will there ever be a real Santa Claus. We see people in Santa suits, but we all know it is make believe.

It is, of course, impossible to return to believing Santa Claus is real.

Likewise, it is blatantly obvious the 'I'/'me' has never been real; the relaxation, the freedom, the utter joy, *of that non-happening or recognition,* is better than any Christmas present imaginable!

Maybe Santa is the recognition of that in which you speak.

Sure. One can keep believing indefinitely.

The self, the 'I 'or 'me' will do anything to keep itself from disappearing.

'This', of course, is not a belief.

It is not possible to return to the illusory belief in an 'I' or a 'me'. Who or what would return and who would be the believer? There was never an 'I' or 'me' there in the first place.

So 'I' or 'me' is a sham?

That could be another word for illusory, if one felt a bit disgruntled with this message.

Cool Night Air

Nothing, lovely nothing, appearing for no one as an apparent nightfall.

Unknowing, wild, meaningless unknowing resonating as indescribable freedom, as an apparent half-moon arcs towards the outline of the apparent Olympic mountains.

What is and is not apparently appearing as a real and unreal body/mind configuration sitting on an apparent chair, writing these apparent words.

Nothing/everything (one word) breathing.

Aliveness appearing as 'This' already; empty/fullness without rhyme or reason.

Unambiguously 'This', adding a blanket to apparent legs, as the cool, apparent night air seeps in.

Discomfort Arises

Discomfort arises.

You really feel that?

Intense discomfort, felt, it seems in the center of the gut, but mysteriously for no one; hence, no judgement, disappointment or interpretation accompanies the pain! Just a flat out, incorruptible bodily sensation, known as a stomach ache, is apparently emerging.

Are you going to take anything for it?

Sipping hot water seems to help. Thoughts arise and dissipate but, strangely, none of them turn into a story of the pain being this, that or the other. There is just pain happening.

What does that feel like to you?

Doubles me over.

I thought, when there's no longer a 'me', pain, at least, would be less.

Sorry to disappoint, but it's probably more. There's no illusory 'self' to shelter in place, with a barricade or protective aegis, to allegedly separate itself from the pain.

Yikes!

Stop it, you're making me laugh.

Laughter.

You asked what I'm going to take for this; well, this is it. Already there is laughter and talking happening. 'This' is it, just this, which is and is not.

Oh, please with the is and is not! I'm concerned about you.

Laughter.

Sure, the individual seems to want to feel good, to feel pleasure and to avoid pain; but when the apparent individual is no more, all the shields, masks and armor created by the illusory me are also no more. Life can sometimes seem to be happening with all in your face, full on, force eight winds.

It's 'This'; simply, unconditional love, wholeness, appearing as any of the five senses, in all manner of apparent pain or pleasure.

No one knows why, for there is no one to know; there is simply 'This' unknowing.

Mysterious huh?

Pain gone?

Appears to be less...

What's strange is the joy that is the pain. Joy and pain seem to be one in the same. Pain is happening, but so is joy simultaneously.

Pain is what is felt, don't get me wrong.

Nothing appearing as pain and joy at the same time?

Yes, apparently.

What do you feel?

Pain.

Do you feel the joy?

No.

You've lost me again.

The joy is not felt or experienced; yet, it is just what is apparently happening. It's miraculous!

Unconditional love appearing as a magical stomach ache?

Laughter.

Round and Round

'Me' dies.

Nothing happens.

It was never there in the first place!

So, it's not really a death for there is not something there to die.

Round and round the apparent 'me' goes, sincerely seeking freedom, love, liberation, illumination; yet, fearing its own death!

Where is this 'me'?

This illusory apparition, this phantom, this ghost, has the gall, the unmitigated gall, to say, "I am real, I can feel it, right here inside this body."

When this 'me' is no more, "Abracadabra," all the alleged religions of the world, spiritual teachers and gurus seem to vanish like dissipating fog from Liberty Bay.

Miraculously, mysteriously, feelings still arise, thoughts, doing all the things that make up a typical human day still happen. Psychological fear seems to vanish. Healthy fear, such as recoiling from an unexpected and sudden close encounter with a wild animal; or dealing with your motorcycle when a front tire blows out at seventy miles per hour, may arise.

The 'I'/'me' wants to take ownership of everything, know it all, experience it all. When that ownership is gone it's not better or worse. Aliveness seems to happen, but splendidly for no one!

There's no one who can help you find this. There's no one that can be of any help whatsoever, because there is no one.

--Sing to the tune of "Pop Goes the Weasel" -- Round and round the apparent world, illusion chased 'This' freedom; illusion thought it was all in fun, but couldn't find what was missing. **POP!** goes the illusion.

See the White Triangle?

Yes, I see it.

You see it, but it's not what it seems to be.

What?

You see it; however, the brain is hallucinating the triangle. There are three 60° angles, and three black circles, each minus a 60° slice, strategically placed on the page. The angles and black partial circles appear as borders that seem to surround the image.

The white triangle is there, but not there!

It's real and unreal simultaneously.

It is and is not.

I just seem to see it?

Correct. When the bordering angles and black partial circles are taken away, a white triangle does not remain. Nothing remains, just white paper is seen. The white triangle was never there in the first place!

My brain creates imaginary borders to complete the white triangle?

Yes, and by the same token, the brain hallucinates and maintains the 'me', the 'I' with its bordering story that seems to begin in early childhood. With the help of its complicit and tenacious partner, the body, felt physical tension locks in the 'I' or 'me' as real.

Take away the apparent bordering body and story and what's left?

Nothing?

Precisely. This sure doesn't help the seeker any, but when the apparent collapse of this hallucination occurs, it is blatantly obvious that there never was an 'I' or a 'me' present in the first place. This purported self is a hallucination, an illusion that is believed as real.

I know what you are going to say, "No one knows this"...

Right! So, it can't be claimed that 'I' did this, for there never was an 'I' in the first place!

The past, present, future, time, space and the body-mind are all part of the never-ending story that act as the defining borders of the 'me', much like the illusory white triangle, which was bordered by the angles and the partial black circles.

The body has a rich, cellular, inherent belief in its own reality; it will, figuratively speaking, constrict into a substance harder than diamonds to support its master-- the brain.

When this apparent constricted energy is apparently released, as it were, nothing remains; however, there is a recognition, so to speak, by no one, of the natural reality, of ineffable freedom, of unconditional love.

There is only wholeness, boundless energy playing, singing, dancing the only song there is and is not, for no one.

Entirely mysterious.

The 'me' is not what it seems.

Love Out of Nothing at All

Unconditional love!

In apparent sickness or health, pain or pleasure, life or death, right or wrong, up or down, unconditional love is what is and is not.

It is what is apparently happening and not happening.

There is nowhere to go, nothing to get, for all is already 'This', with no conditions or stipulations.

'This' is free love, the deepest, most intimate love and it is not now or then.

It is 'This' freedom, 'This' energy, 'This' aliveness. It is all there is and is not.

Whatever arises in whatever form is unconditional love; whether it be a smile or frown, the bliss of a good laugh, or the pain of deep hurt, 'This' love is what is.

It is not something we know, for there is no one to know it. It remains hidden, yet obvious.

Mysterious unknowing?

That can be said, yes.

A freedom so great it can't be described in words?

Sure. Excellent.

Aliveness resonating as nothing and everything?

Absolutely!

No matter what words are used, they are not it, nor can they explain, teach or direct. 'This' freedom, 'This' mystery, 'This' unknowing, 'This' unconditional love is what is and is not.

Love out of nothing at all!

I Don't Know What I'm Talking About

'I' don't know what I'm talking about. 'I' don't know why this is being written. Attempting to convey what cannot be conveyed can be laughable; and, what is being said, doesn't make sense.

When the apparent 'me' died; that was it. The relief of not having to play the make-believe role of 'Jim' any longer was joy beyond imagination; however, to try and tell the apparent story of that disappearance is not possible.

There is not something guiding these apparent fingers as they type, no channeled, mysterious guiding thought, no prior knowledge to be passed on, no miracle discovery, and no spiritually enlightened masters giving guidance. These words simply appear without cause or reason. There is no 'I' who knows anything about anything!

That's pretty much how it has been for most

of this apparent life. The only difference? In the life of 'Jim' there was the constant struggle of somehow convincing the world I did have something to offer, something that could earn money, something others believed 'I' genuinely had.

When the mental and physical rigidity of 'Jim' was no more, so was the need to show others, please others, work for others, do anything for others. It was obvious there were no 'others', just as there was no 'Jim'.

How do 'I' know what I'm talking about?

'I' don't.

The freedom in being able to say it like this is immeasurable. A whole life trying to say it right to survive is gone.

No more ingenious cover letters, resume's, prototypes, interviews, speeches, impressive tools, bosses, colleague's, being the good son, brother or friend.

No more acting.

There is just 'This'. It is not something that remains.

'I' can't say it.

'This'-- which has no appearance.

'This'--beauty that has no form.

'This'-- freedom that is so utterly obvious.

'This'-- which cannot be written down and cannot be spoken.

'This'--noble nothing appearing as:

>   apparent trees and clouds

>   earth meeting apparent sky

>   a slight smile on an apparent face.

These apparent eyes close right now and may never reopen; that would be fine. They do reopen, and that's just fine too.

The mind, undisguised and desireless.

Mine/Thine...gone

Past lives or future lives irrelevant...

All beliefs nonexistent...

The apparent heart beats, the mountains with fresh snow, trees rocking back and forth, fresh air entering the body...aliveness, pulsating aliveness, simply as it is, appearing for no rhyme or reason.

No fear.

No questions.

No problems.

Just 'This', complete unknowing.

Just 'This', wonderfully 'This'.

No now.

No awareness.

No consciousness.

Just 'This'. Enchantingly 'This'.

Beyond imagination.

No space.

No time.

'This' unknowing.

'This' freedom.

'This' aliveness.

The wind whistles, swishes and vibrates, smearing the clouds against the mountains.

The thought arises, "Get in that, go for a walk."

"OK".

An apparent walk happens; yet, there is no outside, no "In it".

No one went for a walk, but there is still breathing hard, shedding a couple layers of clothing to cool off, heat rising from the chest area.

Peaking aliveness.

Whether in fragments or complete sentences, the written word falls short in describing the indescribable, wondrous mystery of unknowing.

How sublime. No longer is there the need to profess or pretend to know anything, especially what is being said in these words. There is just what is happening and not happening for no one.

And, of course, if there is no one writing this, no one will read it.

No one will read it!

Freedom of speech at its peak.

This could be likened to the writings of a dead man; however, there is walking, talking, eating, sleeping, dreaming, exercising, all the cool stuff of a rich, full life.

The illusion of me is no more,

The mythology of death feigned lore?

No Me to Know

Jim, I know there is no 'me', there is an ego here who knows that, who feels that; but I live in a subject/object real world. There is an ego here that wants what you have.

How can something that does not exist know that it does not exist?

'I' have nothing.

I get frustrated and envious of you.

You have everything, a nice house, money in the bank, a beautiful car, luxury trips all over the world, a great family. In short, a lot to lose. The 'me' is afraid. Even though it gets this intellectually, it feels it's going to lose all it has worked so hard to get over an apparent lifetime.

What do I have for you to be envious?

Freedom!

And you don't?

Well, I know I do, and that's the problem.

Knowing?

Yes.

What is being said with this communication is unknowing.

I know and that's just so frustrating.

Laughter

The 'me' thinks that 'This' freedom is going to be an event to end all events; that the universe will open and pour down the divine colors of the Holy Name, Jesus will appear from the clouds, a Bodhi Tree will begin growing in your yard...

Do you think there is an 'I' over here that is free? How could that be?

H-o-w   c-o-u-l-d   t-h-a-t   b-e!?

How do you know this?

I don't know this!

How can you say this then?

I can't! There is simply no 'I' to know anything, nor has there ever been an 'I' to know anything.

Laughter

That's why I'm envious; you (not you) are free of fear.

There is no 'me' who is free of fear.

Do you experience fear?

No. How could I?

No fear at all?

If I swerve to avoid an oncoming car traveling eighty miles per hour in my lane, this body will get an adrenaline rush that could be translated as fear. Natural fear can and does arise.

But you don't fear nuclear war, corrupt government, losing everything?

No. There is no 'I' to fear that; yet, anything is possible. Fear could arise.

That's the kind of freedom I want.

Sorry, you will never get that.

Ever?

Never!

But you (not you) have it.

That which does not exist, will never, ever attain 'This' freedom. How could it? 'This' freedom is already this conversation; it is already anything and everything you have ever wanted. You are missing it via your insatiable appetite to know, to get it, to somehow own rights to nothing and everything. What you are looking for is not even hidden; it is simply 'This'.

'I' don't get 'This', nor do 'I', or could 'I' have it. There is no 'I' to get or have anything.

It always comes back to no 'me' or 'I', and 'This' is all there is and is not.

The Superfluous 'I'

The alleged human being is the only species that has the software, so to speak, to create an illusory self.

Animals are supported by a brain and a body, but they do not create an 'I' or 'me' identity with their brain.

Are animals better off?

You can ask a cat or a dog that question, but, most likely the cat will walk away, or the dog might yawn.

The body of the human supports the 'I' or 'me' as something real.

The body of an animal has no such entity to support.

It sounds like the animal is already in the freedom of which you speak.

Again, you would have to ask the animal.

The human brain is obviously highly sophisticated and clever. Its masterpiece the 'I', 'me', or 'self' appears to outshine nature. It thinks it has conquered the sky, the earth, and perhaps the universe. It thinks it knows knowing. It thinks it knows God.

The human body just does its job. It serves this phantom with an indefatigable obedience. It feels real. It will protect the illusory self with all its power.

Animals protect themselves with all their power.

Yes, and there is no 'I' there doing it. Protection just happens.

Who is better off the human or the animal?

Look at the condition of the human world.

Now have a look at the natural world.

You tell me.

I think I would rather be in the natural world.

The natural world is all there is. The illusory 'I' wants you to see it otherwise. There is 'me' and there's the natural world.

That even sounds ridiculous to me.

It's blatantly obvious there is only what is and is not—the natural world. How could there be a 'me' and then the natural world? My God!

There isn't even a natural world. That concept is a fabrication; just like the 'I' or 'me' is an invention of the brain.

What is real?

Nothing.

No-thing.

What **is,** is 'This'-- unfettered aliveness.

'This' is real and unreal simultaneously. If you could glue real and unreal together and make one word, maybe that would help answer your question.

One thing for certain, most human beings believe the 'I' or 'me' is absolutely real.

You don't?

Laughter.

When the 'I'/'me' is no more, all one can do is laugh when that question is asked; however, laughing seems to make people mad.

There is no 'me' to believe anything.

No you?

No 'you' or 'me'.

Silence.

Wild

How about that!

There's no having to get anything.

No having to wake up after years of religious, spiritual or meditative practice.

Who is going to wake up?

There is no who to wake up!

There is no 'I' or 'me' to wake up.

The seeker can ask, "Am I aware?", pause and get a verification every time of "yes, I am aware".

This is a strong verification that the 'I'/'me' is safely intact, that there really is an 'I' in there that can be aware, that is aware and waking up. Complete dualism!

There is just 'This' freedom, magnificently hidden from the 'I'/'me' character.

Conversely, 'This' freedom (for lack of a better

word) is utterly obvious for no one.

Hidden in separation, yet, obvious in wholeness?

Yes.

There's no 'me' sitting here realizing something. Just wholeness, unconditional, impersonal love, arising.

Nothing and everything (one word) just as it naturally is and is not (one word).

Nothing to gain or lose?

'This', which is unconditional love, is always already; even using words like always and already imply dualism. No. Nothing to gain or lose.

There is no 'I' sitting in it, aware or present in it. 'I' is separation and separation is illusory. The 'I' will never quit searching. To quit searching means death for the 'I'.

There is sitting, writing, aliveness resonating

with apparent energy that is entirely inexplicable.

What is apparently happening is not happening in space or time. 'I 'or 'me' does not get that, nor can it figure it out, or make sense of it; yet, there is a recognition of 'This' the natural reality.

Who or what recognizes the natural reality?

It sounds funny to say it this way, but no one recognizes the natural reality. The natural reality is and is not. There is nothing to recognize 'This' or 'That' which is always already the case.

So, how do you know this is true?

I don't.

There is no 'I' and no truth to be known.

'This' **unknowing** is life at its most dangerous.

No protection.

Bare.

Sans filters or guides!

It is absolute death to the illusory self, which is a laughable statement; there can't be a death to something that does not exist!

To live in 'This' fullness sounds wild.

Well said.

'This' wild aliveness,

'This' resonating beauty of unknowing shines with apparent light and color;

'This' sings with the intimate sounds of water over rocks and the wind through the trees.

Life full on. No 'I' or 'me' to interpret, justify or rationalize. A tornado of fire and ice, a tsunami toppling the Everest of the 'self', without the slightest hesitation, figuratively speaking.

No more questions.

No more searching,

No more, "Something is missing."

Just 'This', as it is already.

Just 'This', empty fullness for no apparent reason.

Just 'This', simply 'This', freely 'This'.

Boundless freedom, ringing, singing, dancing, laughing, crying,

"This is it!"

To write of 'This' freedom is like trying to describe the heavy mist moving horizontally across the distant trees. Utterly impossible!

So why do you write?

'I' don't.

Writing happens.

For who?

For no one.

No God to Pray To?

There are no words to describe 'This' aliveness.

Seeing happens, but it really does not, because there is no one who sees. It is, therefore, impossible to describe what is apparently seen by no one.

Nothing, no-thing, is real, yet, unreal simultaneously.

'This' nothing is everything.

No one knows 'This'

Huh?

Unknowing resonates as alive, pulsating energy without cause or effect.,

Can you clarify that?

No.

It is impossible to describe nothing being

everything. It, and it's not an it, is all there is and is not.

How can you say that?

'I' cannot!

No one knows 'This'.

There is no 'me' to know.

'I' don't say 'This'.

No, 'I' to be 'am'?

Precisely!

No God to pray to?

God is not being denied; but who would pray? Do you see?

Absolutely hopeless...

Absolutely hopeless...for there is no one to have hope.

Anything and everything is 'This' already.

It is 'This'.

Not out there.

Not in here.

Simply 'This'.

Mercifully 'This'.

Unconditionally 'This'.

No ups or downs, rights or wrongs, longs or shorts.

Only 'This', which is nothing appearing as everything.

Again, how do you know that?

I don't.

Then why are you saying it?

I'm not!

There is no 'I' here or there, in or out period! There is no objective case 'me' or nominative case 'I' period!

The subject 'I' is but a dream, illusory, made

up from early childhood. It believes it is real and, of course, wants to live. It is thwarted repeatedly on its futile quest to survive in a world comprised of other illusory 'me'(s), who all seem to be playing the *who is smarter* game.

That which tries so hard to fit in, survive, be liked, loved or recognized, is no more and, what's more, it never was in the first place!

There is simply 'This' which is indescribable. The search is over, but, it was never there in the first place.

I don't get it!

Of course you don't. There's nothing to get and no 'you' to get it.

Mist Moving Through Distant Trees

'This' is it...

A slight mist moving horizontally through distant trees gives way to a dissipating rainbow.

Hot tea, thoughts, sitting.

The face is flat, the usual buzzing in the head, the heater flips on.

A deep breath, a sniffle.

Everything happening, yet, there is no 'me'!

Nothing is happening!

There is no revelation, or need, or want or desire to share this. Who would share and with whom?

The snow leopard and wolverine seem to be my apparent friends. Solo creatures surviving in rough, remote terrain, simply living. Free aliveness, thriving in what appears to be insurmountable odds, in the natural world.

The human seems to have even more to surmount, given he or she thinks and appears to be trapped in the physical rigidity of 'me'. The human being must deal with an apparent past and future, that is glorified in every respect possible, and enhanced by out of control technology!

Stooped with the weight of 'me', most of the population of the apparent world, carry this load to the grave.

Who would want this 'me'?

It seems everyone! Yet, when it is recognized, by no one, that the 'me' has no actual existence, the question arises: how could anyone have ever believed there was a 'me' in the first place?

Light, color, sound, movement are what is and is not, and cannot be explained.

That's Enough!

The apparent cry of the world.

We can't take it anymore.

The game continues.

I'm scared.

Of what?

The horror we see every day on the news.

Can you stop watching the news?

I need to be informed.

The 'me' is afraid of its own creation, now it wants to do something about it. It will protest, sit in, use social media, join causes, go to war.

The 'me' refuses to see that the complication is the 'me' or 'I' itself!

The 'me' causes perplexing predicaments, then it wants to fix its unsolvable mishaps with better thinking and action.

...but I think I can make a difference!

How can something that has no actual existence make a difference?

'You' believe in your own reality, as do millions, billons of others. You verify your illusory reality because so many others agree with you; the more seeming agreement, the stronger your reality.

No 'me', no agreement.

No agreement, no illusion.

No illusion, no separation.

The apparent natural world is free of 'me'; however, there is still struggle, fighting and survival. Birds and animals do not have to intellectually agree with each other. There is simply a natural order to things, and there is no natural world separate from the world of 'me'.

Wholeness, oneness is the natural world. The 'me' just thinks it is separate and can do something about the apparent problems it creates.

You're saying the problem is the 'me'?

Yes, the <u>'me'</u> **is** the problem.

'Me' believes in the horrendous condition of the world **it** created; now it wants to do something about it. How witty...

No 'me', no complications.

It's just **so** obvious, but when the human believes he/she is this rogue-phantom 'me'...

World leaders believe they are this 'me'.

Yes, and look at what they are saying and doing.

Spiritual leaders?

Providing complicated rules to that which has no complications sound free?

There is just 'This', inexplicable unknowing free of words such as time and space.

You can't tell me there is no space.

You can't tell the 'me' anything. There is no 'me'!

No 'me', no space.

How can you say that?

'I' can't say that. How many ways can it be said? There is no 'me', there is no 'I', and there certainly is no 'you'.

Who is saying what is being said?

Words, phrases and sentences appear or arise from nothing. One could say no-thing; however, there is no ownership of this apparent communication. There is no 'I' or 'me' saying this is true or not true.

Maybe it is freedom speaking, but that turns into an idea or concept open to interpretation and judgement.

Perhaps the joy of what is and is not gives voice to the simplicity of unknowing.

There is just unknowing. There is no "who" saying anything.

The freedom...the freedom!

If the 'me' could only say, "That's enough," to its apparent illusory nature...

Alas, it cannot make itself into a reality. An illusion is just not what it seems. Seeing apparent

water on what is only sand will not help quench
the thirst of a bone-dry throat.

Steel gray sky

cold

snow in the forecast

the wonder

the joy of 'This' aliveness

arises as a slight smile

gazing into the unknown.

Free Fall

I love to travel, eat in expensive restaurants, socialize, drive fast...

Will I lose my desire for these things if the 'me' drops away?

Yes, but guess what? The apparent 'you' will do everything you seemed to do before, even more, because there will be no one there to say you can't.

I free fell in a bungee jump once, before the apparent collapse of the 'I'/'me'. The hard part began when the jump master said, "Three". There was only two and then one left. When he said one, it was *over the edge hard* time.

In that one second, of apparent time, there were at least a dozen thoughts as to why I should not step off that platform; every one of them logical and reasonable, believe me!

"Two, keep looking at the horizon Jim,"

exclaimed the jumpmaster.

"Am I glad I recently used the restroom," was my only thought.

"One," said the jumpmaster.

My arms went horizontal, as if I was going to flap hard and fly.

The body tipped forward slightly and...

A rush of air and a grin...no thoughts, no nothing.

Nothing is the closest I can come to describing that fall.

I could go into detail about coming to the end of the rope; however, to try and describe the free fall is impossible.

I've heard some people describe everything and nothing as freefall, just aliveness in freefall.

Try to imagine riding that hot Ducati *Monster* without the filters of ego.

I can't imagine that.

That which is and is not comes under that same category of unimaginable. All the cool stuff still happens, yes, but for no one.

Well, what's the thrill if there's no one there?

There isn't, but all the apparent thrill still arises in a body without the 'I'/'me' riding along.

Freefall, my man, freefall!

So, nothing happens when the me collapses?

Nothing happens. Very good!

How could anything happen? There's nothing there in the first place for anything to happen.

No Answers

What happens when you're down, feeling low, it's raining, your nose is running, nothing is going the way you want it to, you're alone, your body aches, you're feeling stupid, you don't want to do anything?

Wow, well said! You have it, that's it. That's what's happening.

...but

What do you want me to say, something that will make it better?

Laughter

Oh, you're just going to laugh at me?

Laughter

How could it get any better than this! You are describing what is apparently happening perfectly.

Oh, you're a cruel person!

Look at me, I'm suffering here.

Where is this 'me' that appears to be suffering?

Right here, right here!

OK, there's laughter happening from what you say is "Right here". So, now we can add laughter to what is apparently happening.

Oh, oh...

Laughter.

So, I'm just supposed to feel terrible and laugh about it?

Laughter

I don't know. There are no answers, but the honesty in this conversation is engaging.

So, you can't help me?

No, I can't help you.

Then, what's the point in what you are talking about?

No point, and there is nothing being talked about. There is no 'me' over here talking to a 'you' over there. There is just what is apparently happening, and that which is not happening.

It's that enigmatic not happening that confuses me.

The 'me' will never know what is not, but as long as the 'me' remains intact, it will certainly keep searching for what it can't know.

Ya' don't budge do ya'?

Who is there to budge?

Laughter

Is there a lot of smiling apparently happening right now?

Yes.

That's what's happening and what is not happening. Useless to try and figure this out.

This unconditional love apparently shows up as *feeling bad* the apparent 'you' described so eloquently. That's what is happening and what is not happening for no one.

Well, I feel it!

Of course, you do. The 'me' loves its story and the more down, it can apparently become, the safer it remains. This is 'my' runny nose, 'my' aches and pains, 'my' depression...

The story of 'my' misery?

The story of 'your' misery. The 'me' has a story and the story has a 'me'.

You mean if there is no 'me' there is no feeling lousy?

Sorry to have to say, but the body can feel even worse, because the protective bark, so to speak, the barricades and filters created by the illusory 'me' are gone.

So, there's just sitting and suffering?

No suffering. Who would suffer? Just all those ailments you mentioned arise in the body, but for no one.

How about the accompanying thoughts?

Thoughts arise as usual, but for no one. No story takes hold. The body aches, the nose runs, thoughts arise of every sort, but don't stick, as it were, to anything.

So, how do I get rid of this 'me'?

'You' can't because 'you' do not exist. How can something that does not exist get rid of anything, including the seeming cold that 'you' apparently have?

What can I do?

Drink lots of liquids, get plenty of sleep, stay warm, and call a doctor if your symptoms worsen.

Laughter

Soaring

There is no learning to fly; yet, there is apparent flying.

Free falling, rising, floating.

'This' aliveness, 'This' freedom seeming to drop as sadness and rise as joy.

Can it drop as joy?

Ever drop straight down in a roller coaster?

Scary and exhilarating simultaneously!

Yes.

'This' wild energy can appear as dazzling light, glowing twilight, shady dusk and pitch-black darkness. The metaphor of darkness and light easily translates into happy or sad, pain or pleasure; yet, the flight of life happens, it just is as it is. When there is pain it hurts, when there is pleasure, apparent contentment.

When the 'I'/'me' disappears, nothing changes in the way the apparent human engages with the apparent world; however, it does seem to be a tad more intense or a bit more relaxed.

All the feelings, emotions, and thoughts rise and fall, come and go, drift with the wind...

Nothing, complete, wonderful unknowing magically, mysteriously appearing as these newly formed words dancing across a white background on an apparent sheet of paper.

No rhyme or reason.

Nothing and everything.

Wholeness, without cause or effect, appearing to happen neither here nor there, up or down, right or left, now or then...

Simply 'This'.

'This' is what's happening. Not for 'me' or 'you' or 'anyone' for any reason.

Just soaring?

Sure!

Aliveness apparently rises from a tiny mote in an invisible updraft.

What is and is not dives into a vertical, heart in throat, straight down free fall.

Boundless love floats untethered by apparent time or space.

Rising, falling, floating...

Rising, falling, floating...

Soaring, drifting, gliding as the joy of unknowing.

Wings of nothing catch unseen currents of uncompromising gladness.

Floating, rejoicing in the unseen skies of that which is and is not.

Naturally 'This'

Breathing

Electric-swooshing-ringing between the ears.

Body sensations.

Thoughts arising and dissipating for no one.

No 'me', 'I' or 'self'.

Just 'This'...

Natural being.

Sitting, writing, hearing, seeing.

No story.

Just 'This', simply 'This'.

Nothing appearing as everything

for no reason.

Wild, chaotic energy appearing in every
conceivable form.

Beyond imagination.

Inexplicable, unconditional nothing appearing to constrict into an illusory 'I'/'me' in billions of human forms.

A mystery for no one.

So plain, obvious and free.

Impossible to find, impossible to learn, impossible to know.

Just 'This'!

Nothing and everything simultaneously.

Wholeness appearing as separation.

No in here or out there.

Just 'This'—freedom.

just 'This'—unknowing.

just 'This'-- unconditional love.

Just 'This'-- timeless, space less, dimensionless no-thing writing.

Everything the apparent somebody always wanted, always dreamed of, always desired, yearned for, longed for is 'This' already.

Not hidden.

Obvious.

Not clear or unclear, for clarity has nothing to do with what already is everything. There is no 'me' to be clear or unclear, present or absent, here or now. How could there be, when all there is, is 'This'?

No need to clarify or explain, for who would be here or there to have something clarified? There are no 'others' just as there is no 'me'. To clarify is to teach and because there is nothing to teach, because there is nothing to learn, it is impossible to know why oneness, wholeness simply appears for no reason.

Gift or No Gift?

So, breathe easy, 'This' is all there is and is not; miraculously impossible to get or understand. Unknowing could be likened to an apparent gift of freedom. The apparent gift of nothing could look like the apparent gift of everything. The apparent gift of what is not, could appear to be the gift of what is.

...but really, there is no gift. Who, or what would be the giver? Likewise, who or what would be the receiver? If, even, there could be an apparent gift, it would be 'This' which is already the case.

This is kind of like our "Do you still believe Santa Claus is real?" discussion.

Yes.

Laughter

You can't see it.

Right, who or what would there be to see?

Yes, it's just simply 'This'. Anything is possible.

No seer?

No seer. Simply 'This'. Apparent words being read, apparent thoughts, apparent seeing.

So mysterious!

For no one.

Unknowing!

Laughter

Unknowing.

Laughter

'This' is unknowable; yet, thoughts and questions arise for he or she who searches and purports a want, a desire to know; but falsely, for if the seeker could receive this...

It would mean spot on death?

Exactly, figuratively speaking.

Kind of like, this unknowing is not this unknowing?

Words appear and seem to point, but that is dualism.

Right, who or what could point?

Yes, the 'self', the 'I', the 'me' is illusory! So really, nothing can be said.

I like all the words and talk.

Right, all those words and talk keep the 'I'/'me' safe; but watch it, this communication illuminates the hopeless, futile chase of that which is not real seeking fulfillment and wholeness.

This disclosure lights up the fact, that the 'I'/'me' construct is **illusory**.

That sounds like the gift!

Apparently.

A Reflected Sunset

An apparent sunset reflected through a porch sliding glass door appears. Mountains shaded with pinkish, lavender clouds, the sound of a car, the buzzing in the head, icing the knee, forming words on apparent paper...

A spectrum of red, orange, pink and lavender fill the sky which is seemingly on fire.

The haunting, simple, probing ring, of an apparent bird called the Varied Thrush, articulates the quiet, still forest.

No 'I', or 'me' to interpret or explain this natural reality, perfect in every detail, reflected through a porch door window!

Simply 'This', mysterious, joyous freedom of unknowing, as the apparent sun slips gently behind the seeming mountain named The Brothers.

What the 'I' or 'me' has needed, longed for,

prayed for, lived for is 'This' already.

No 'I'.

Just 'This'.

No 'me'.

Ineffable freedom.

No 'I' or' me'.

'This' aliveness.

No 'Jim'.

Nothing happening.

No 'self'.

The natural realty appearing as 'This'.

Free

There is nothing to get from this disclosure, nothing to understand.

It is just obvious there is no 'I' or 'me' to get anything.

No 'I' or 'me' hears this communication. How can you hear unknowing?

Hearing is a tricky word, because the brain can't hear what is being talked about in this message. The illusory 'me' can say it understands or gets it, but there is nothing to get. When seeming hearing happens, there is no longer an 'I' or 'me' present to say it hears what is being said or talked about.

When the apparent 'Jim' *heard* this message, there was getting up from a chair and walking through the kitchen. There was no 'Jim' to know 'he' was walking through the kitchen.

It was not an understanding.

It was not enlightenment.

It was not liberation.

What could be understood, enlightened or liberated?

Nothing.

Nothing.

Nothing.

The spellbinder exposed.

'This' mysterious unknowing shines.

Who or what hears this message?

Nothing!

'I' can't hear this message?

There is no 'I' to hear it.

But 'I' can when the 'I' goes away

It doesn't go away. It was never there in the first place. Remember, this is dualistic language trying to describe the indescribable.

When the word *hear* is suggested, it is implied that a recognition seems to happen.

There is a recognition by no one that loving freedom is all there is and is not.

Laughter, apparent empty space, silence, well-being, peace, joy or happiness could be words used to describe 'This', the simple wonder of what is and is not.

Free!

Wind Through Trees

Constant, outward movement seems to be happening outside. Trees in ostensible, perpetual motion, gracefully dancing; it is what is apparently happening.

The sound of the wind through the trees is constant, strong, organic and powerful; yet, indescribable.

Hearing 'This' is no one. Seeing 'This' is no one. Movement, sound, light and color arising out of nothing! The seeming wind is 'This', an invisible force, pushing and shoving all in its apparent path.

'This' is beyond description as the phenomenon of apparent wind cuts a concealed swath through a myriad of trees on a winter day.

'This' is unknowing, as an apparent hawk tries to hold it together and passes quickly across the skyline.

'This' is nothing and everything, as apparent whitish, grey clouds move fast across patches of blue sky.

'This' is what's happening; apparent sitting, words appearing on a computer screen, the heater clicking on, the sound of the washing machine in the apartment above me.

It sounds so simple!

Unequivocal simplicity!

I get it when you say, "Wind through the trees" because that's what is.

But when you say, "It's also what isn't," that confuses me.

Apparent wind through trees appearing out of nothing. Nothing and everything is said as one word; just as what is and what isn't is said as one word. There isn't a something that comes from a nothing. There are not two ever!

You can't know that. What is there to know?

Nothing?

That could be said, but, of course, that wouldn't be it either.

I know, I know, because it's not an "It".

The wonder and awe of the wind through trees gives way slightly to blue sky brimming with bright sunlight.

That's just what's apparently happening.

Yes! There is no one who knows what 'This' is and is not. How utterly spectacular!

For nobody?

For nobody, exactly.

Just 'This', plainly 'This' radiating aliveness, for no reason.

The seeming sky darkens, slight movement with the trees, a fly lands on the wall, a car blasts up the hill...

Yes, but there are things going on all over the

world you are not aware of.

There is no 'me' to be aware of something here, let alone a 'world' out there!

Aren't you aware of the wind through trees?

There is seeming wind through trees; yet, no one is aware. What is being advocated in this conversation is a mystery.

I want to solve the mystery!

There you go again, thinking you are actually real and that you can do something about unknowing.

You sound like an existential nihilist.

There is no belief or philosophy in this communication to imply that anything is wrong or needs to be changed. There is not one word that sees life as essentially meaningless or hollow; that one reject religion or belief in a higher power; that one essentially drops out of society to live a life free from all rules.

'This', is not a belief. 'This', which is everything already, is what philosophies, religions, and scientists are seemingly looking for. Simply 'This' ordinary causeless freedom happening.

Aliveness arises for no one.

Here and now, right?

No here and now. There would have to be something separate in a here and now; something that would know there is a here and a now; a 'me' or an 'I' to know there is a here and a now.

There is, most excellently, nothing abstracted from wholeness.

The wind through the trees is all there is and is not.

Thank you!

Joshua Aaron Galbraith for the laughter we enjoy in the freedom of unknowing.

Nanette Wilson for playing *the devil's advocate*. You are that special friend a fortunate few meet once in an apparent lifetime.

Tony Parsons, Jim Newman and Andreas Muller. Your voices are heard—apparently.

Darryl Elves for your unconditional, supportive friendship.

Bonnie Tabb for giving of your precious time in helping me with computer issues.

About the Author

Jim Galbraith, a native of the Pacific Northwest, was born in Washington State, and educated at Lewis and Clark College in Portland, Oregon.

When he was seventy, while sitting at his dining room table, life, as he knew it, disappeared.

Strangely, as he walked through the kitchen, moments later, there was no sense of a separate inside self perceiving a separate outside world. Inner and outer seemed to be one organic whole.

Stoic, firm non-experiential seriousness ensued; something unknown, but familiar, seemed to resonate as unconditional and timeless.

It was, as if, death was occurring, or perhaps, this was its aftermath; yet, breathing and smiling was happening!

All that seemed to be known had disappeared.

The brain was lucid, the body intact, but 'Jim' was gone. There was nothing left; yet, everything remained!

Aliveness was all there was, and peculiarly, all there was not.

Jim has not reappeared.

The Freedom of Unknowing is his first book.

The Freedom of Unknowing

P.O. Box 2696

Poulsbo, WA 98370-9998

United States

Printed in Great Britain
by Amazon

53363547R00088